HAPPY CUSTOMERS FASTER CASH

Eastern Europe chapters

A guide to effective communication in financial Customer Relationship Management

Andriy Sichka

Marcel Wiedenbrugge - Cliff Wynn

Cover design: Patrick van der Doef

Preface Eastern Europe edition

This edition of "Happy Customers faster Cash" is intended to combine the idea of financial Customer Relationship Management (fCRM) with the customs, cultural features and conditions of doing business in Eastern Europe. It is mainly relevant for Belarus, Moldova, Russia and Ukraine. The cultural features could also be useful for other countries that emerged from the former Soviet Union.

Eastern Europe is the region where the traditions of business commenced or, it could be better to say, re-commenced their development about 25 years ago after the collapse of the Soviet Union. At first, the vast majority, if not all business transactions were made on cash terms, financed by bank loans available at extremely high interest rates. At the beginning of the 21st century, with the introduction of international companies into the market place, companies started to grant credit to their customers to support trade and to gain a competitive advantage.

Though the majority of practicing managers, especially in finance, tend to consider accounts receivable as a 'necessary evil' and perceive customers as 'debtors', establishment of a strong longstanding relationship with key customers is not something new in this profession. Sales and marketing representatives, who communicate with customers regularly, know the value of good customer relationship management very well. We believe this book will help to enhance collaboration between suppliers and customers with additional support from the side of finance and credit management.

Dealing with overdue or outstanding invoices and attempts to reduce them as much as possible is a very important task for any business. Though usage of strict, conservative credit policies on risky markets could be justified, tight control and strict collection procedures are limited in their capacity to improve business results. Moreover, excessive or even aggressive actions may negatively affect customers' loyalty and lead to the loss of sales and revenues. In contrast, sustaining positive cooperation with customers and having a constant readiness to provide support not only improves payment behaviour, but also opens the door to business growth.

In "Happy Customers Faster Cash" we address everyone working in the process of managing credit and communication with customers i.e. credit controllers and credit managers, finance, customer service and sales staff. Owners of small and medium size enterprises, whose business significantly depends on customer relations, could find this sound advice very useful as well.

I hope this book will provide you with a better understanding of practicing an effective and customer-oriented approach to corporate credit management in general and Eastern Europe in particular.

Andriy Sichka

CONTENTS

1. CREDIT MANAGEMENT IN EASTERN EUROPE

1.1 Credit Management in Eastern Europe

The following chapter does not pretend to be a comprehensive analysis of credit management in the region. Instead, its intention is to give you an idea about the features of operations in the area and to provide some useful information about the availability of different credit auxiliary services.

The history of the region includes almost 74 years of the Soviet Union, between 1917 and 1991, when all enterprises were the property of the state and any sort of private business was illegal. Due to this, the spirit and the culture of entrepreneurship in Eastern Europe has existed for only a relatively short period of time. The region, therefore, still has significant scope for further development in terms of free market thinking and entrepreneurship.

In this context credit management is not an exception. For a substantial period after 1991, companies had very limited trust in each other and were delivering goods and services mainly on cash-in-advance terms. Granting of credit to customers in the B2B segment has only started to become systematic in the late 1990-s.

The initial source of professional expertise in credit management was subsidiaries of international companies, who brought specialist knowledge and higher requirements to credit management. As a result local personnel became more knowledgeable and professional standards were raised to a higher level. In addition to that, the recently set up Association of Credit for Central and Eastern Europe and Russia's Institute of Credit Management are becoming drivers in the development and promotion of the profession.

Credit management has very good prospects in Eastern Europe because of the following two key factors. Firstly, demand for professional credit management is growing. According to research from Coface Russia 79.2% of companies regularly extend credit terms to their customers and another 14.1% do so from time to time. Secondly, local people are well known for their abilities to work hard and learn quickly. Without doubt, credit management could reach global standards in a very short period of time.

Perception of credit management

In general, credit management is not perceived as a separate profession or business function, with the exception of financial services. Even the term 'credit' itself is associated more with bank loans by the vast majority of people working in business. Therefore, some Eastern European companies offering their goods and services on open account terms do not consider this as credit.

Parallel to that, in local subsidiaries of international companies and many large(r) local companies, people who are responsible for credit/accounts receivable are usually part of the finance department. However, the job title 'credit manager' can be found more and more often on both companies' organisation charts and openings in the job market, especially in Russia and Ukraine.

The risky market environment and relatively low margins created a demand for strict credit control and debt collection. Constant focus on these two tasks is the main cause of a negative perception of credit with colleagues from other departments, including general management. As in other parts of the world, this constitutes the basis for the professional conflict between sales and credit personnel.

On the other hand, many credit managers, and especially those who have been working in the profession for a few years, extend their services beyond the basic tasks and are highly appreciated by members of other teams and customers. Positive practices, such as regular meetings between sales and credit, joint business reviews and customer visits are becoming more and more common practice.

Credit policies

Companies operating in the Business-To-Business (B2B) sector usually have a set of general business rules on how to grant credit and setting/determining payment terms. However, having a written credit policy as a separate document is currently not common for many businesses in Eastern Europe.

Where they are in place, written policies tend to be strict and conservative. Often their provisions include collateral as a condition of credit extension and the requirement to contact the customer immediately upon the detection of overdue invoices.

At the same time, a substantial number of companies trade with their customers on open terms without doing a credit check or credit risk assessment. Instead, many of them rely more on the customers' reputation and (past) payment behaviour.

The authority to make credit decisions generally belongs to higher management in both local and international companies. This could be the finance director, the general manager or the business owner in small and medium sized companies.

Payment methods

For the B2B segment in Eastern Europe a bank transfer is the preferred payment method, covering 95% of all financial transactions. An Electronic Payment System operated by the domestic National Central Banks carries out transfers between banks. These systems work equally well in all four countries and are very fast. Payments transferred in the morning usually reach the supplier's bank account by noon or at least within the same working day. Payments transferred after mid-day, usually arrive by the evening or the next morning. If a payment promised by a customer does not arrive the next day – it may either have not been executed properly or it could be a sign that the customer has cash difficulties. The transfer time for payments within the same bank is normally a couple of hours maximum.

Among other factors, fast payment processing is a consequence of high competition in the financial markets. For example, according to the National Bank of Ukraine the total number of banking institutions in the country is 163 and the Central Bank of the Russian Federation confirms 830 active institutions as of January 2015.

Local legislation sets very low limits for cash transactions between companies. Though technically possible, this method brings the additional risk of robbery and therefore it is not widely used. The above factors make it difficult to use cash on delivery and similar terms in trade.

Payment terms

In contrast with the European Union, where the Late Payment Directive was adopted in 2011, legislation of Eastern European countries does not impose a maximum length of payment terms. In other words it could be any payment period agreed by the parties to a contract.

In practice domestic B2B terms vary from 3 to 60 calendar days. Short payment terms and long transportation distances give ground to the custom of counting the payment term and due date from actual arrival of the goods and not from the shipment or order entry date. Despite the fact that it gives rise to disputes concerning deliveries, such an approach is definitely justified, particularly given the huge territory of Russia, where transportation of goods can easily take one week and even longer.

So called single-date terms, where all deliveries for the month are payable at one specific date, are mostly used in consumer operations and are hardly found in B2B. Equally, early payment options are not widely used and are perceived as difficult to administer.

The length of the payment period depends on the kind of industry, type of product and bargaining capacity of the company. Large customers, for example key retail chains, do not hesitate to use their commercial position and negotiation power in order to get longer payment terms. At the same time, retail chains, especially international ones, are usually low risk profile customers. It is also worth mentioning that retailers, being cash rich, are more disciplined payers than wholesalers and distributors.

Cash in advance or prepayment terms are not widely used and incur a high cost of financing. Thus the application of such terms is often accompanied by a substantial price reduction.

Late payment is not something unusual, therefore actual collection periods are often longer than the agreed upon term, which also depends on the strength of the suppliers' credit policy. Though legislation in all the countries provides for interest fees for late payment, they are rarely applied unless a supplier is ready to bring a case to court. Customers are usually very reluctant to recognise invoices for late payment interest, therefore in resolution of payment related issues suppliers try not to generate additional problems and damage relations. By contrast, the amounts of court claims contain full late payment fees.

Many suppliers, especially production companies, have developed so called 'distribution programs' where a customer receives a retrospective bonus for the accomplishment of certain conditions. These conditions normally include accurate, on time, payment for deliveries. Such programs have proved to be an effective method to encourage on time payments from customers, where the bonus paid under such a program represents a substantial part of the customers' profit.

Credit Checks and Credit Information

As already mentioned, the majority of decision-makers prefer to rely on their customers' payment history and tenure of the relationship. In addition to that, before entering into a contract with a substantial value, companies usually request recommendations/references from the personal network of directors and/or business owners. Among companies and banks across the region, it is quite common for them to create their own security service or department. Usually former state police or security officers head these departments. Responsibilities of these groups include the verification of the customer's business reputation. In banks the head of security is also a member of credit committee.

Similarly to some other regions in the world, (e.g. Middle East countries), the practice of sharing financial information is rather the exception than the rule in all four countries. Moreover, audited financial statements, with the obvious exceptions for public companies, are in most cases not available. Though companies are used to providing their financial statements to the banks as part of a normal process of obtaining loans and other types of financing, they are usually very reluctant to disclose financial statements and other financial information to trade creditors. Such an attitude is generally explained by the protection of commercial secrets. Taking into account the significant number of crimes against businesses in the past, especially in the 1990s, this behaviour is understandable.

Credit reference agencies usually use the financial information obtained from state run statistical institutions, where all companies should deposit their financial statement as a requirement of the law. Though this is still useful information for the purpose of conducting a credit check, financial statements are neither verified by the authorities nor by independent auditors in the vast majority of cases. Please refer to the credit services section in chapter 1.3.1.

Debt Collection and Court Recovery

Bigger companies, especially in the financial sector, usually set up in-house collections departments and services. Very often, collection of outstanding amounts is a part of the responsibilities of the security and legal departments.

To date, most Debt Collection Agencies (DCAs) are involved in the recovery of consumer debts for banks and insurance companies. The practice of purchasing financially distressed portfolios by DCAs from banks is also quite common, but for consumer loans only. Although many of the DCAs in the region do offer recovery of corporate debts, it is only about 20 percent of their business.

The service of debt recovery through the court system is provided across the region by DCAs, law firms and independent lawyers. Court systems in all four countries have a lot of similarities. For example to attend a court hearing as an official representative it is not necessary to be a qualified barrister, however a degree in law is usually expected as a matter of practice. Specialisation of firms and lawyers in debt recovery is rather unusual.

The limitation period for court claims is in general 3 years in all four countries. However, it could vary significantly depending on the type of the debt. For example in the Republic of Belarus claims related to bills of exchange are limited to six months and the period for claiming outstanding loans is 5 years. In practice, however, cases where the creditor lost the right to claim the debt are very rare. The typical time to consider the court option does, in general, not exceed 90 days overdue, which is considerably shorter than the legal limitations.

The number of successful recoveries in the B2B segment does not seem very high, because of the two following reasons:

- From the point of local trade customs, bringing a case to court often means a serious disruption of the relationship with the customer or even the loss of them. Companies, therefore, apply the court option as late as possible in the case of a commercial and/or financial dispute.
- Debtors often have no assets to repay the debt by the time of the court hearing.

Despite the general background, each and every case will be different and special. Therefore the support of a professional domestic lawyer would be very advisable in order to avoid unnecessary difficulties, especially if you have to go to court.

With some minor domestic variations, the court procedures are the same across the region. A court's order, in the case of favourable decision, goes to a debtor's bankers for execution. If after a reasonable amount of time a claim has not been satisfied, a creditor can ask the court to turn the order onto the property of a debtor. The court's decision to do so is executed by the Court Executional Service, which is a part of the court's administration.

As a general rule, physical possession of the goods places the customer in a far stronger position than the legal title to them. Especially in cases where the distribution of goods does not require their special registration, for example fast moving consumer goods or commodities in the domestic market. Therefore it is advisable to include a retention of title or a similar clause into a contract with a customer, however, the practical application of this would take additional administrative effort.

In all cases it is very important to remember, that utilisation of the court option is a serious step which generally leads to a termination of all relations with a customer. Such options should only be used as 'last resort', when you have tried all other means and do not see any other solution.

Use of credit management software and technology

Due to the early stage of development of the credit industry in the region, the demand for specialised credit software is currently very low. Some of the bigger banks and international companies use dedicated credit and collections software, which is mostly purchased at a corporate level via their headquarters.

Local companies use either existing international software for credit and collection operations, or order bespoke solutions from domestic software companies. Though Eastern Europe is famous for its IT specialists, specialisation of local companies on credit risk, accounts receivable control and collections software is still yet to happen.

1.2 Useful links about credit management, doing business and business culture in Eastern Europe

Credit Management Services

Country Risk Reports

Atradius is global credit insurer. An overview of country risk reports, including Russia, can be found here: http://global.atradius.com/ccriskreport/list/ccriskreport.html

Coface is a global credit insurer sharing country risk information on its web-site. www.coface.com/Economic-Studies-and-Country-Risks

Euler Hermes is another global insurer who shares country ratings: www.eulerhermes.com/economic-research/Pages/Interactive-country-risk-map.aspx

Trading Economies is a useful resource, which provides country ratings by Moody's, S&P and Fitch: http://www.tradingeconomics.com/country-list/rating

Country risk reports of Belarus, Russia and Ukraine. http://www3.ambest.com/ratings/cr/crisk.aspx

Credit Insurance

ICISA is the International Credit Insurance Surety Association www.icisa.org Under "Publication" you can download the Yearbook 2014/2015, which provides a global overview of credit insurance companies and in which countries they are active. The main credit insurance companies active in Russia are: Atradius (in cooperation with a local partner), Coface, Credimundi and Euler Hermes. For Belarus, Moldova and Ukraine no information is available. Credit insurance companies often conduct economic research, so it is useful to check the websites of credit insurance companies regularly.

Local Export Credit Agencies:
Russia. Agency for Export Credit Insurance: www.exiar.ru
Ukraine. JSC State Export-Import Bank of Ukraine: www.eximb.com
Belarus. Beleximgarant: www.eximgarant.by

Credit Rating Agencies

Russia
RusRating: www.rusrating.ru/en/index.php

Ukraine
Credit Rating: www.credit-rating.ua/

Credit Reports

Credit Information Providers with regional coverage:

Dun and Bradstreet: www.dnb.com

Coface Debt Collection: www.coface.com

Professional Partner: www.propartner.ee

Interfax: www.spark-interfax.ru

Local providers:

Russia and Belarus
OOO Creditreform-Rus: www.creditreform-rus.ru

Ukraine
Creditreform Ukraine: www.creditreform.ua

Debt Collection

The Atradius Debt Collection Handbook (8th edition)

This handbook contains detailed information on debt collection procedures, rules and regulations in 38 countries, including Belarus, Moldova, Russia and Ukraine.
www.atradiuscollections.com/global

Economic research "International debt collection – The Good, The Bad and the Ugly", in which debt collection in 44 countries is (briefly) analyzed including Russia.

www.eulerhermes.com/mediacenter/Lists/mediacenter-documents/Economic-Outlook-International-Debt-Collection-1213-dec14.pdf

Providers with regional coverage:

Atradius Debt Collection www.atradiuscollections.com/global

Coface Debt Collection: www.coface.com

Professional Partner: www.propartner.ee

Local providers:

Russia and Belarus
OOO Creditreform-Rus: www.creditreform-rus.ru

Ukraine
Creditreform Ukraine: www.creditreform.ua

Verdict Collection Company Ltd.: www.verdict.kiev.ua

Moldova
IM "INCASO" SRL: www.incasso.md
PfB Collecting: www.pfbc.md

Doing business, business culture and credit management

Business culture and etiquette

Russia
www.cyborlink.com/besite/russia.htm

Ukraine
www.tryukraine.com/society/business_culture.shtml

Belarus
www.belarus.by/en/business/business-customs

Moldova
http://guide.culturecrossing.net/basics_business_student.php?id=136

Credit Management Associations

Association of Credit for Central and Eastern Europe (ACCEE): www.creditcee.eu

Russia's Institute of Credit Management (RuICM): www.ruicm.ru (in Russian language only)

Doing business in Belarus, Moldova, Russia and Ukraine – country guides

Doing Business 2015 guide published by the World Bank. A complete source of information comparing business regulations for domestic firms in 189 economies including Belarus, Moldova, Russia and Ukraine.
www.doingbusiness.org

The Worldbank database. http://data.worldbank.org

Factoring

The Association of Factoring Companies (AFC) - professional associations of market participants factoring in the Russian Federation.
http://asfact.ru

Payment behaviour

Credit insurance companies have a reasonably good insight into the payment behaviour of companies in most economies. Especially Atradius and Coface sometimes publish corporate payment survey results. Occasionally D&B also publishes corporate payment studies.

To get a general impression about payment behaviour in Russia, check this document.
www.informadb.pt/biblioteca/ficheiros/27_payment_study_2013.pdf

Check your local credit information provider or credit insurance company for the latest data.

European Payment Report
A survey about payment behaviour and payment risks in Europe, conducted in 29 countries (B2B and B2C) including Russia.
http://www.intrum.com/press-and-publications/european-payment-report/

Payment systems and methods

Insightful information regarding local payment systems can be found on the National Payment System pages of local central banks' web-sites:

The Central Bank of the Russian Federation: www.cbr.ru/eng

The National Bank of Ukraine: http://bank.gov.ua/control/en

The National Bank of the Republic of Belarus: www.nbrb.by/engl

The National Bank of Moldova: www.bnm.md/en/about_bnm

A global database of (electronic) payment providers and payment methods.
www.about-payments.com/knowledge-base

2. COMMUNICATION WITH THE CUSTOMER

2. Communication with the customer

2.1 Slavic culture and communication in credit management

As already mentioned in chapter 1.3, the culture of Eastern Europe was heavily affected by the long communist era when nearly everything was controlled and owned by the state. The transition to a society in which the individual takes responsibility is not yet complete. This however is already less relevant for the younger generation, who grew up in an environment that has more resemblance with democracy as practiced in the West.

Over its history, the USSR contained about 100 different ethnic nations, which continue to exist in the newly created states. In addition to Slavic people (Russian, Ukrainian, Belarusian, Moldovan) who historically speak Russian as a mother tongue or second language at least, there are Hebrew, Tatars, and a large group of Caucasian and North Eastern nations. In the vast majority of cases people from ethnic groups try to keep together by preserving their national language, culture and, of course, religion. While Orthodox Christians represent the majority of the population, Judaism, Islam and many other religions are actively cultivated and practiced.

Taking into account the number different nations, explanation of all the cultural differences would require a separate book. Those involved in business in the region, in 80% of cases one will deal with Slavic, Russian-speaking people, so the following section is especially dedicated to them. It would also be highly advisable to ask local people about the customs and traditions of a specific ethnic group in case you have to deal with them.

Also, it is always good to remember that irrespective of ethnic, religious and language backgrounds, all people are different. Keep in mind that in dealing with people, we first of all always communicate with an individual personality. Cultural authenticity gives us only a general idea about our counterpart, which is useful in the beginning. Effective professional communication, however, is something to be built by personal interaction.

Slavic people in general

Internationally, Slavic people are known for their directness, sincerity, hospitality, but they can also be a bit impractical.

Slightly similar to the Dutch culture, the Slavic culture prefers open and clear communication in order to avoid unnecessary complications. People usually talk to each other in a sincere and direct manner. "No" usually literally means no, and "yes" usually literally means yes. Sincerity of the culture does not restrict or discourage people to express their emotions. People normally perceive discreet behaviour with distrust, as if a person is trying to hide something. On the other hand, an open style of communication may look friendly and pragmatic, but in difficult or stressful situations it could be perceived as rude or even aggressive, especially in comparison with Western and Far East cultures. However, what people may perceive as aggressive is to Eastern European people nothing more than a frankly expressed opinion. Strong emotions are normally shown in relation to special circumstances or difficult situations and almost never against you personally. If your customer is emotional during a call, just accept it and be honest and sincere in your response.

Another degree of directness is taking things literally. By contrast with Western languages, which contain up to 50 percent of expressions with figurative meaning, 90 percent of expressions in Russian are those of direct literal meaning. Even when people speak English very well, they naturally understand the literal meaning of the words. Thus, asking, "how are you" be ready to hear either "why are you asking?" or you will hear a long detailed story about all kinds of trouble that has happened to the person in last couple of weeks. Time is treated in a similar way. For example if you say "...in half an hour", people normally expect a promised action or result in about 30 minutes. Moreover, expressions like 'at some future time' may be perceived negatively if used for something important or urgent. In other words, be explicit and precise and stick to your promise.

The tradition to treat guests well has deep historical roots. Nowadays it is mostly reflected in food and drinks. As matter of tradition, the inviting party normally pays for everything. It is presumed, however, that the invited party will come back with a similar invitation at some future time. Ladies are always an exception and gentlemen are usually expected to pay for ladies, irrespective of the type of relationship.

When communicating with customers and resolving credit issues, it would be advisable to:

- Always keep in mind the literal meaning of what has been agreed with a customer and ask for clarification if you are unsure.
- Make sure you are on the same page with your customer. For example: "Do I understand you correctly – due date March 31st means that money would be in our bank account by the end of the working day March 31st?
- Do not react emotionally where your customer raises his/her voice, try your best to stay calm and constructive.
- Always be consistent with what and by when you promised to do some action. Should you have difficulties to comply, inform your customer or stakeholder as soon as possible
- Try to be open and honest as much as possible. Especially in cases where the dispute is clearly caused by your company. Recognition of your own mistakes and faults produces much better results, than attempting to avoid responsibility.

Rules and regulations

Though the application of law, in general, has a strict and literal character, people are used to looking for a back door. Corruption may still be an issue and rules may be interpreted differently in particular situations. In terms of business this would have a paradoxical meaning that literal compliance to the law does not necessarily guarantee you are safe: the authorities might punish you even for small, unimportant non-compliance.

It is highly advisable to pay as much attention as possible to all documents related to taxes. Tax representatives in the region have a high authority and are used to being very strict towards taxpayers. You can expect that every little mistake a business makes will be treated in favour of the state.

It is just as obvious, that such an environment affects relations between a customer and a supplier. Documents accompanying the delivery of goods or services rendered are also the basis for the calculation of taxes and could be seriously scrutinised by the authorities. Mistakes in such documents may lead to substantial issues on the customers' side. Cases where taxes were increased after audit by tax authorities are common.

Thus, maintaining the high quality of documents given to customers adds a lot to the positive image of your company. Furthermore, readiness to correct or redo them when it is necessary to help a customer helps to significantly affirm relations.

Politics and religion

The history of the region contains a lot of controversial events, which can be perceived differently by people from outside the region. The political positions of people working together could be completely opposite. Very often political events have a connection with religion. As such it is best to avoid these topics in business conversations, as it can easily lead to conflicts and escalations. It is highly advisable to keep conversations to business and small talk.

Effective Communication in credit management

One of the key features of the region is the fast changing business environment. Because of this people carry out operations in a very fast manner and normally do not plan their activities too far in advance. This has implications on business communication in general and obviously on credit management in particular.

In most cases the collection of overdue invoices and dispute resolution is part of sales people's responsibilities. In this case sales personnel play the role of account management, so a customer has a single point of contact for every issue. Though it might be perceived as a 'sales monopoly' on customer relationship management, having good relations with sales, could prove useful when trying to improve payment behaviour. It goes without saying that credit managers have to allocate substantial time and effort to build good working relationships with sales. Customer contacts by credit team members should be aligned with sales upfront. It is also a good idea to visit customers together with sales representatives.

Contact with customers usually takes place by phone. For more important issues, face to face contact is more effective. Written communication is used only in such cases where it is important to have a record in writing and where legislation requires you to do so. Generally, the telephone is the preferred means of communication for all kinds of credit management matters, though it is always practical to send the customer a short summary of a call by e-mail.

In such an environment the ability to communicate effectively is paramount. Based on practical experience it would be advisable to:

- Avoid small talk if you are calling your customer or another counter-party on an urgent matter and go straight to the point

- Be clear about what you want and be ready to explain it in simple words. Always start your explanation with what you want and then explain why (if your counter-party is ready to give what you ask for, there is no need for explanation)

- Never refuse to cooperate, be flexible, but take a pause to think if the situation goes beyond your authority

The establishment and maintenance of effective communication with the customer is very important in any part of the world. In Eastern Europe, where trust and collaboration are derived directly from personal contact, it becomes paramount. Therefore time and effort spent on the development of business relationships with customers will never be wasted.

12 excuses for late payment and how to deal with them

Below we have listed 12 excuses. We will discuss each excuse in detail, provide an example and show you how to deal effectively with each excuse.

1. *We never received the invoice*
2. *We always pay our invoices after 60 days*
3. *I just paid the invoice*
4. *I really don't understand it. I paid a few days ago*
5. *The payment has not been authorized, because the person responsible for approving invoices (departmental manager or general manager) is not available/out of the office.*
6. *We never received the goods*
7. *My customer has not paid me yet*
8. *The invoice was incorrect and I am still waiting for a credit note*
9. *The order was cancelled*
10. *My customer went bankrupt.*
11. *The financial paperwork is at my accountant's office.*
12. *The managing director is on vacation and he needs to approve the payment.*

EXCUSE #1

Customer: *'We never received the invoice.'*

Supplier: *'If I send you a copy by email today, can you organise payment to us before Friday?* [If there is a reason to doubt the customer's statement, you can indirectly indicate that not receiving an invoice is a very rare event, so the customer will have to think of another excuse in the future]

Explanation

This excuse is frequently used and may be true. Although delivery times may vary from country to country and guarantees of delivery are not provided, most post ultimately arrives at its destination. If it is a particularly high value or important invoice you may want check your local postal service for estimated delivery times, traceability and possibly use a guaranteed and signed for delivery service.

A customer who claims that he did not receive the invoice, often, but not always, means that the customer has lost the invoice or incorrectly 'filed' the invoice (i.e. the invoice lies somewhere in the proverbial pile of documents to be processed, in other words the administration is probably a mess). If you notice that the same customer frequently uses this excuse, it is a good idea to monitor the customer more closely. So for future deliveries you could contact the customer a few days after the delivery took place to check if the customer has received the invoice. If the customer wants to know the reason for your call, you can tell him that it is important to you that invoices are produced promptly and arrive addressed to the correct person. After all, it is important for both the customer and the supplier that invoices are correct and sent in a timely manner. By dealing with the situation in this way, you will leave a professional impression, improve customer experience and, over time, it may lead to improved payment behaviour by your customer.

EXCUSE #2

Customer: *'We always pay our invoices after 60 days.'*

Supplier: *'I hear what you are saying, but, our terms and conditions clearly state that your payment terms are 30 days net and you know that. I would like to talk to you about how we can prevent these payment issues in the future?'* Alternative: *'I hear what you are saying, but how would you feel if I bought goods from you on 30 days net, but then paid after 60 days?'* [wait for their response and then dig deeper into the topic]

Explanation

Customers can sometimes be very creative by inventing their own payment terms. The explanation for such behaviour is not always clear, but often these types of customers think that they are so important to a supplier that they will be happy to do business with them no matter what payment terms they might invent. In such cases it can be very difficult to get the customer back in line again. On the one hand it would not be fair to allow one or a few customers to have different, more favourable terms, but on the other hand you may not want to offend the customer and possibly lose their business. It takes patience and a clear strategy, to know what to do with such customers. Therefore you need to understand the future commercial importance of such customers and discuss how to proceed with the sales department. Changing payment behaviour is often a time consuming process. Being consistent and reminding the customer of the terms in a friendly way will maintain the relationship and may improve payment behaviour. However, if this doesn't work you need to decide, in conjunction with sales, whether to continue the customer relationship or gradually say goodbye.

EXCUSE #3

Customer: *'I just paid the invoice'*

Jenkins: *'That's good news. Did you pay the invoice electronically?'* [wait for a reply] *'When exactly did you pay the invoice (or outstanding amount)?'* [wait for a reply]. Alternative: *'How much did you pay and to which bank account?'* [wait for a reply]? *'If you paid yesterday, it should be visible on our statement tomorrow at the latest. I will check then, thanks for your time.'*

Explanation

This reply is probably the one you will hear the most and it is very easy for the customer to use. However, you can easily check if the customer is telling you the truth or not. A payment processed by the customer cannot be reversed, unless the bank refuses to execute the transaction due to lack of funds or insufficient credit. During the conversation, you don't need to tell the customer you will contact him again if you do not receive the payment within one or two days. You will contact the customer anyway if the payment doesn't show up on your bank statement. When a customer uses this excuse often it may indicate that you are dealing with an undisciplined or unorganised customer. It may also mean that they are in a poor financial position, so when in doubt you better check their creditworthiness. With these types of customers it is important to stay in close control and send reminders shortly after the due date. A proactive, but customer-friendly, reminder strategy may work as well. Credit management software and automated collections strategies can obviously help a lot to improve payment behaviour.

HINT

If you ask the customer to send a copy or print screen of the electronic payment, be aware that the payment has actually been processed, so the customer cannot delete the payment instruction afterwards. However, a payment that has been instructed does not necessarily mean that the payment is processed. If the credit limit or overdraft facility of your customer with his bank has been exceeded, the bank may decide not to execute the payment instruction. One of the fastest and most reliable ways of getting paid is by phone payment (telephone banking), where your bank confirms receipt of the payment via email or by telephone.

EXCUSE #4

Customer: '*I really don't understand it. I paid a few days ago.*'

Jenkins: '*A couple of days ago I talked to you and you told me that you paid the outstanding invoice/invoices. What has happened, did the bank not process your payment?*' [wait for a reply] '*Well, if you could arrange a payment today we can clear the account.*' [optional] '*Could you telephone me when you have processed the payment and I can check our account to confirm receipt of the payment? Is that OK with you?*' [wait for a reply] '*Great, I look forward to receiving the payment. I hope you have a good day and I am pleased we could resolve this issue.*'

Explanation

If you have to call the customer because he did not meet his commitment to pay you on a specific date, it usually means one of two things:

1) The customer simply did not make the payment

2) The bank has not approved the payment instruction due to a negative balance or other financial problems with the customer.

The first case suggests that you are dealing with a lazy or unreliable customer. The second case may mean that your customer has liquidity or cash flow problems, so you also need to check the creditworthiness of the customer. If your customer faces financial troubles he is unlikely to tell his suppliers about it. At the same time, it can be a huge relief for the customer if he knows that his supplier is willing to listen to him and think about ways to resolve the problem. Especially when financial problems are temporary, it can help both the customer and the supplier to openly discuss the matter, so you can both find practical and realistic solutions.

Also, don't forget to inform the sales department, so that they know what going on as well. In both cases it is important to monitor the customer closely over the next few months and find a way to improve their payment behaviour.

EXCUSE #5

Customer: '*The payment has not been authorised, because the person responsible for approving invoices (departmental manager, procurement manager or general manager) is not available/out of the office.*'

Jenkins: '*I thought that you were responsible for all payment processes? Who needs to authorise this invoice and when will they be back?*' [wait for a reply] '*Does this mean that future payments will be delayed?*' [wait for a reply] '*I am not very pleased about this. The invoices are well overdue, so we need (stronger: have to) to find a solution today. Can you contact your colleague who can authorise payments, I will call you at [time] to see where we go from here. Is that OK?*' [wait for a reply]

Explanation

Hiding behind decision makers or procedures is something you will find in all kinds of organisations, especially within larger ones. Just when you need person X, he is not there or in a meeting. Large companies often work with so called payment procedures as a part of the procurement process. The invoice may be authorised, but when payment isn't, you still won't get your money. In practice it is very tough, if not impossible, to bypass these procedures. The best thing you can do is to build a good relationship with your contact in the accounts payable department. It will probably not change the authorisation procedure, but you may get a higher priority on the list of suppliers. It depends on the commercial and strategic importance of a customer as to what measures and adjustments of collections strategies you need to consider when this problem occurs often.

HINT /TIP 1

Sometimes it can be very hard to get hold of someone by phone to talk about outstanding invoices. In these situations it may help to let a colleague from sales or account management call the customer and ask for the same person. Customers with liquidity problems often don't like to talk about it. However, business does go on, so when your customers depend on deliveries for their own business to continue, they will still want to talk to people from sales. Once your sales or account manager has your contact on the line, he can easily put them through to credit management. Therefore a good relationship between sales and credit management is essential, so you can team up if required.

HINT /TIP 2

If you suspect that you are being fobbed off, because your contact is hard to get on the phone, then you may have to try alternative methods. Maybe the secretary is blocking you from talking to the managing director. In this situation it is important to stay in close control and get the secretary 'involved' in your goal. A very simple but effective method is asking direct questions, such as: 'When did you see or talk to Mr. X' or 'Did you pass on my message to Mr. X.? What did he say?' or 'Why did Mr. X. not call me?' By asking these types of questions it will become more difficult for the secretary to maintain her role of protecting her boss. Remember to stay friendly and asking the right questions can be a very effective way to get to where you want to be; in this scenario you want to talk to the managing director.

ATTENTION! Regarding payment issues, liquidity or cash flow problems, be aware that you **do not** discuss these with anyone other than your accounts payable contact at the customer. Payment problems can sometimes be very sensitive and if the boss is your contact, he will probably not appreciate it if you discuss the company's financial problems with one of his employees. So always be discrete when you talk about late payments or overdue invoices.

EXCUSE #6

Customer: *'We never received the goods!'*

Jenkins: *'I will immediately check with despatch, one moment please.'* [call despatch and ask if they can confirm the delivery and can send a copy of a signed delivery note]. *'If you didn't receive the goods, did your receive the invoice?'* [If the answer is yes.] *'Why didn't you contact us earlier, as I assume that you needed the goods you ordered?'* [wait for a reply] (meanwhile you have received a copy of the signed delivery note from the despatch department). *'I just received a signed copy of the delivery note, which proves that you have received and signed for the goods. I will email a copy of the delivery note to you now, so you can have a look at it and check internally. I will give you a call in an hour, so we can discuss payment of the outstanding amount?'* [wait for a reply]

Explanation

Every new customer should receive a copy of your terms and conditions. In these terms there is usually a section about non delivery or disputes and how to deal with them. This should include a time period in which claims for non or short delivery should be notified to the supplier. So a customer claiming that they have not received the goods, while having received the invoice, is actually breaking the terms and conditions. It may also indicate poor administration and handling of incoming goods at your customer. If this excuse is used often by the same customer, then it is advisable to monitor the customer more closely with regard to confirmation of receipt of goods.

It may be worth asking your despatch department to call them after the next few deliveries to confirm with them that the correct quantity and type of goods have been received.

HINT

When the goods arrive at the customer a delivery note needs to be signed, but also make sure that the name of the recipient is clearly readable (preferably get them to print their name underneath the signature). In practice and in particular when the driver is in a hurry the (electronic) delivery note often only has a (digital) signature but does not mention a name. When a delivery is disputed, it can save a lot of time if the name of the recipient is clear. Instruct your drivers or give clear instructions to your external logistics partner.

EXCUSE #7

Customer: *'My customer has not paid me yet.'*

Jenkins: *'I am sorry to hear that, but does that mean that you can't pay any invoices anymore?'* [wait for a reply]? *'Of course it is frustrating that your customer hasn't paid you, but I am afraid that this is no excuse not to pay us. Can you make a payment today?'* [wait for a reply] *'When do you expect your customer to pay you?'* [wait for a reply]. [Alternative 1]: *'We have to pay our suppliers and employees on time, so it is important that our customers pay us on time.'* [Alternative 2, if nothing else works] *'OK, as soon as you receive payment from your customer, which you are expecting on* [date expected payment], *can we agree that you will immediately pay the outstanding invoice(s).'* [wait for confirmation].

Explanation

This excuse is not only a poor one, but from a customer's point of view it is not a very smart one either. Often this excuse is an indication that your customer is experiencing liquidity or cash flow problems. It may also say something about his credit management policy. However, if you have a good relationship with your customer you should be able to discuss the issue openly and work on a practical solution. If progress is a bit sluggish, you could always try to turn the situation around and ask the customer how he would feel or act if he was in your position (tip 24). By confronting the customer with his own excuse, he will see that it is ineffective and harms him more than it helps him.

When the customer tells you that he expects his customer to pay soon and then he will be able to pay you, and if the invoice is not seriously overdue, you may accept this. Accepting this kind of excuse should be an exception, so you don't give your customer the idea that he can get away with it every time, by establishing a precedent. When this kind of excuse is used frequently by the same customer, always check the creditworthiness of the customer and discuss this with sales.

EXCUSE #8

Customer: '*The invoice was incorrect and I am still waiting for a credit note.*'

Jenkins: '*What exactly is wrong with the invoice?*' [wait for a reply] In this case it seems that the wrong discount was applied: 5% when it should have been 15%. '*When did you realise this mistake?*' [wait for a reply] or '*Why didn't you let us know earlier, because now the invoice is now overdue?*' [wait for a reply] '*Surely you check the invoice on receipt? It is common practice to notify us of any problems with invoices within five working days, so maybe in future you could let us know as soon as possible. I will make sure that you receive a credit note and a correct invoice as soon as possible and check our systems to make sure that this does not happen again. I will let you know when the credit note and the new invoice are processed, so you can arrange immediate payment. Is that OK with you?*' [wait for a reply]

Explanation

Queries regarding incorrect invoices, deliveries or damaged goods should always take place within the timescale as stated in your terms and conditions. Since queries regarding incorrect invoices, prices or discounts, are frequently made after the invoice is due for payment it is important to pay extra attention to this category. In contrast, in the case of incorrect deliveries your customer will most likely call you the same day. Of course it can sometimes happen that the customer forgets to let you know. Always check if claims for incorrect deliveries are valid or not and conduct analysis afterwards. Ultimately any claims should be kept to a minimum, as they have a negative impact on the business process, costs, cash flow and the customer relationship. If claims are made frequently and after the invoice is due, it is a good idea to temporarily check new deliveries and invoices as soon as they have taken place. Also discuss the matter with sales and logistics.

EXCUSE #9

Customer: '*The order was cancelled.*'

Jenkins: '*I can't see any notification on our system. Who did you discuss this with and when?*' [wait for a reply]. '*Did you cancel the order by telephone or in writing?*' [wait for a reply]. [Where the customer informs you long after the delivery was made] '*Why didn't you call us as soon as you received the goods?*'[wait for a reply]. '*One moment please, I will contact our sales department.*' [following the conversation]. '*I just spoke with our sales department and they haven't received any cancellation of the order. Before I make a decision, I would like to discuss it with your account manager and then call you back to finalise the matter. Is that ok with you?*'

After talking to the account manager, it appears that he knows nothing about the cancellation either. The order was placed at the customer's office and signed by him. The account manager decides that this order should not be taken back. You call the customer back.

'*I have talked to* [name account manager], *and he confirmed that you placed and signed the order at your office. This means that the order and delivery is valid and that the invoice should be paid.'* [wait for a reply]. In this case the customer accepts the position. *'Now that we have resolved the problem would you arrange payment of the outstanding invoice this week?'*

Explanation

It happens to all of us that we sometimes make a mistake or that the market suddenly changes and as a result we have to cancel an order. It can also happen that a supplier sometimes ships an order that was previously cancelled by the customer. No matter what the reason, the customer needs to communicate incorrectly delivered orders or the delivery of cancelled orders in a timely manner. A good customer relationship can be very helpful, but prerequisites are transparency, honesty and timely communication from both sides. If the customer just responds when the supplier calls him chasing an overdue invoice, then you could say the customer has acted negligently. The standard rule is that any shipped order that has not been queried within a couple of days of delivery, should be considered a normal fulfilled order that has to be paid for within the usual terms.

On the other hand, don't play hard ball unnecessarily when the customer has accidentally made a mistake. Especially in cases where cancellation of an order is a rare event, don't make too much fuss about it and simply give in to the customers' wishes. Being flexible and bearing the costs of picking up the goods often benefits the customer relationship and future sales. Always make sure that your customers know how to act when they need to cancel an order and also instruct your sales people, so they can inform the customer as well.

Also make sure that your business processes and procedures are robust and easy to understand, so you will avoid unnecessary mistakes. This is usually a joint effort between sales, logistics, finance, credit management, service and IT. By efficiently working together, you can save a lot of time and costs, which benefits both the supplier and the customer.

EXCUSE #10

Customer: *'My customer went bankrupt.'*

Jenkins: *'I am sorry to hear that. What does this mean for your organisation?'* [wait for a reply] *'How did this happen? Were you taken by surprise?'* [the answer will give you more of an insight into the quality of your customer's credit (risk) management] *'I understand it must be very inconvenient and difficult for you, but if you went bankrupt tomorrow, should I tell my suppliers that I can't pay them for the time being?'* [wait for a reply] *'Despite your current cash flow problems, it is important that we find a solution. When do you expect to be able to pay?'* [wait for a reply] *'Two months? That seems a bit of a long time to me. I would suggest a payment plan/schedule, where you will pay* [amount part payment] *for the next (number of) weeks.'* [optional] *'Until you have fully paid the outstanding amount we are happy to ship new orders against advance payment.'*

Explanation

If a client of your customer goes bankrupt this could have a temporary negative impact on your customer's liquidity. Although a bankruptcy cannot always be predicted, it may say something about the quality and consistency of your customer's credit management and the way they monitor the creditworthiness of their customers. If a bankruptcy seriously impacts your customers liquidity or capacity to pay, this is an indication that your customer's financial status and liquidity is not very strong and you need to be more alert with this customer or issue a new credit check. A bankruptcy is of course an unpleasant and sometimes costly experience, but with proper credit (risk) management in place you should not experience this too often and it should not significantly impact a company's capacity to pay. A customer who tells you that due to the bankruptcy of one of his customers he cannot pay you, actually reveals more about his financial status and creditworthiness than he may realise.

EXCUSE #11
Customer: '*The financial paperwork is at my accountant's office.*'

Jenkins: '*When will your accountant return the paperwork?*' [wait for a reply] '*In two weeks? Can I suggest that since the invoices are well overdue, I send you a copy of them by email, so you can arrange payment today? Is that alright with you?*' [wait for a reply]

Explanation
This excuse can't be used by the customer too often. After all, how many times a year do you visit your bookkeeper or accountant and leave all your paperwork? Using this excuse implies that your customer would also not be able to pay his other suppliers, which is quite unlikely. When used more frequently, it is often an indication of financial problems. The best way to deal with this excuse is to send the customer a copy of the invoice(s) and ask him to pay immediately. If the customer still refuses to cooperate, you can always tell the customer that slow payment may delay new deliveries or in the worst case put the customer on stop.

EXCUSE #12

Customer: '*The managing director is on holiday and he needs to approve the payment.*'

Jenkins: '*When will your MD return?*' [wait for a reply] '*And does this mean that you can't pay other suppliers as well?*' [wait for a reply] '*Unfortunately, since the outstanding invoices are seriously overdue, if you cannot arrange payment all shipments may be delayed.*' [this is a friendly way of saying that the customer is put on delivery hold/stop]. '*How can we resolve this problem?*'[wait for a reply]? If the customer doesn't want to cooperate, you can apply more pressure. '*I really don't want to put you on stop, but you leave me no choice unless you pay the overdue invoices. I hope you understand my position. If you can pay earlier, please give me a call. Otherwise I would suggest you make an urgent payment as soon as your MD has returned from his holiday.*' [wait for a reply] '*OK I will contact you on* [the date the MD returns], so we can resolve the matter.*'

Explanation

A managing director who 'suddenly' goes on holiday and doesn't leave clear instructions for his staff, or doesn't authorise one or two employees to make payments is, in fact, an example of poor management. It is not only bad to act like this, but it also leaves a bad impression about the mentality of their supplier (relationship) management. It is also bad for the employees, because they are not able to resolve financial matters if required. This is clearly not the way to do business and a chat with the managing director when he returns from holiday wouldn't hurt. In a good and productive customer relationship, it should be possible to say that you are not pleased with this kind of behaviour. Prevention is always best, so pay a bit more attention to your customers before the holiday season starts and make clear arrangements with your customers about payments during the holidays so you can avoid the situation described above.

Dealing with late payment excuses.

The schedule below may be helpful in showing how you can deal with excuses for late payment. With a lot of practice and listening to your customers and colleagues, you will automatically learn how to deal with almost any excuse in an effective and customer-friendly way.

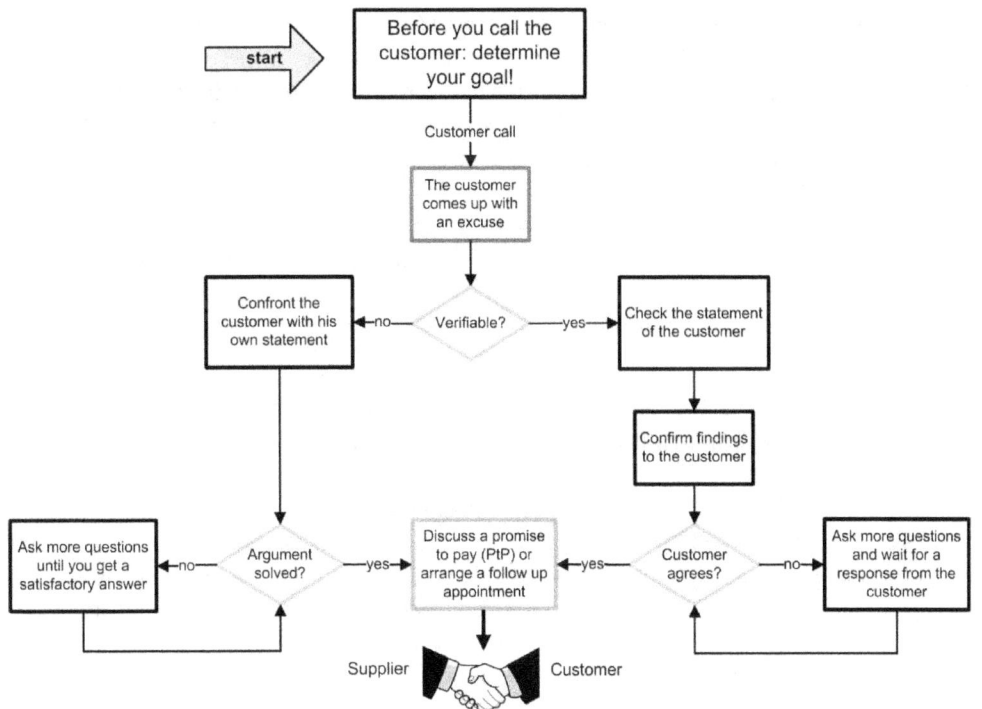

Figure 1: Flowchart dealing with excuses

The authors

Andriy Sichka

Andriy Sichka is an international credit manager with many years of business experience. He is managing partner in A. Sichka Consulting and Development Director of the Association of Credit for Central and Eastern Europe (www.creditcee.eu). Andriy successfully accomplished training and consulting projects in companies such as JT International, Electrolux and Golder Electronics.

He is a member of the Chartered Institute of Credit Management and the Association of International Credit Directors.

www.creditengineering.com
andriy.sichka@creditengineering.com

Marcel Wiedenbrugge

Marcel Wiedenbrugge is managing director of WCMConsult. Marcel combines knowledge and experience in account management/sales, credit management, service management and related software solutions. In the past he worked for companies like Ricoh, Van Ommeren Ceteco, PCD Polymere and Yamaha Musical Instruments Europe.
Most of the time he worked in a B2B environment, but he is also quite familiar with retail. Marcel is an entrepreneur, speaker, writer, researcher, trainer and consultant. He develops, organizes and conducts workshops, trainings and seminars. He frequently writes articles and is the author of several books.

www.wcmconsult.com   marcel.wiedenbrugge@wcmconsult.com

Cliff Wynn

Cliff Wynn is managing director of RK Business Training Ltd. Cliff has both experience of working in the training, collections and tracing industry for many years. He has also worked with and for many of the leading professional bodies within the credit and collections industry, including the role of Head of Training for the Institute of Credit Management. He has built up a considerable knowledge of running a training business plus has 'hands on' experience of telephone and doorstep collections, compliance, consumer credit licence applications and tracing. During his career Cliff has worked with many large organisations on various training programmes in the collections area. Clients have included, Orange, Shell, Marston Group, Brighthouse, NPower, British Gas, Polycom BV, and the Finance and Leasing Association.

www.rkbusinesstraining.co.uk   cliff@rkbusinesstraining.co.uk

Notes

Notes

www.ingramcontent.com/pod-product-compliance
Lightning Source LLC
Chambersburg PA
CBHW070754180526
45168CB00004B/1608